LEVEL 2 READER

Snow Babies

By
Joan Emerson

Scholastic Inc.

PHOTO CREDITS:

Photos ©: cover main: Jenny E. Ross/Corbis Images; cover top: CG Textures;
back cover: DLILLC/Corbis Images; 1 main: Jenny E. Ross/Corbis Images;
1 top: CG Textures; 2 top left and throughout: FotoShoot/iStockphoto;
2 top right and throughout: loops7/iStockphoto; 2 bottom right and throughout:
brainmaster/iStockphoto; 2–3 background: Jari Paananen/CG Textures;
3 top: Daisy Gilardini/Getty Images; 3 center and throughout: AndreaAstes/
iStockphoto; 4 background and throughout: Jari Paananen/CG Textures;
5: AlaskaStockRM/All Canada Photo; 6: Barcroft Media/Getty Images;
9: Paul Nicklen/Getty Images; 10 top and throughout: brainmaster/iStockphoto;
10 main: Minden Pictures/Superstock, Inc.; 13: age fotostock/Superstock, Inc.;
14: Rex Features/AP Images; 17: Mandi Miles/123RF; 18: Johnny Johnson/Animals
Animals; 21: Andrey Zvoznikov/Ardea/Biosphoto; 22: KeithSzafranski/iStockphoto;
25: Rich Kirchner/Photoshot; 26: Eric Baccega/Nature Picture Library;
29: Eric Isselee/123RF; 30: Jean-Louis Klein & Marie-Luce Hubert/Science Source.

ISBN 978-0-545-85228-9

10 9 8 7 6 5 4 3 2 1   15 16 17 18 19 20/0

Printed in China   68
First printing, September 2015

Designer: Marissa Asuncion
Photo Editor: Alan Gottlieb

INTRODUCTION

animal babies live all over the world. Some animal babies live in the snow, on the ice, and in chilly waters, where the temperatures are freezing. It would be too cold for you to visit, but their bodies are built to keep them safe from the icy weather. Read on to explore the amazing wintry world of snow babies!

sea OTTER

Sea otters give birth in the water, immediately introducing their pups to the cold Arctic Ocean. For weeks, mothers float on their backs while holding their pups close to their chests like a hug! Soon, the pups learn to swim and hunt for food. After eating, the otters clean their coats. This helps them stay **water-repellent**, which keeps them warm.

When sea otters sleep, they sometimes hold hands so that they won't float away from one another!

POLAR BEAR

Polar bears live on the ice sheets and in the freezing waters of the Arctic, one of the coldest places on the planet! A polar bear mother gives birth to a cub in a den, which she creates by digging into a big pile of snow. Cubs are born with thick fur on top of a layer of fat to keep them warm. On the bottom of their paws is more fur to help them grip the slippery ice.

Polar bears may look cute, but they are some of the most ferocious animals on Earth!

narwhal

narwhals are related to whales, but they have one very special difference! The narwhal is famous for the 8-foot-long tooth that grows out from its jaw. This tooth looks a lot like a unicorn's horn, so the narwhal is often called "the unicorn of the sea"! They are easy to spot since they swim in the Arctic Ocean in **pods** of fifteen to twenty narwhals.

Some scientists think the narwhal uses its long tooth to sense changes in water temperature, but no one knows for sure!

ARCTIC HARE

arctic hares live in the North American tundra, an area that is known for its below-freezing temperatures. The arctic hare is bigger and fluffier than a pet rabbit, and it has a snow-white fur coat to keep it warm. This white coat also helps to **camouflage** it from danger. When the snow melts in the spring, the fur changes colors to blend into the rocky landscape.

Arctic hares like to stick together—they've been found hanging out in groups of more than 1,000 hares!

ALASKAN HUSKY

Alaskan huskies are best known as sled dogs. In the past, when travel was hard in the snowy winters, Alaskans would use dogs to pull their sleds from one place to the next. They needed a **breed** like the husky, which is strong and can stay warm for hours outside. Today, Alaskans have a famous 1,000-mile race, called the Iditarod, which pits human **mushers** and their teams of 16 dogs against the wilderness.

> **The Iditarod race can take on average from 9 to 15 days!**

Snow Leopard

Born in the chilly mountains of Central Asia, the snow leopard is the ultimate winter warrior. It has a thick and fluffy fur coat to keep it warm and can also use its tail, which is nearly the size of its entire body, as a scarf! Plus, snow leopard cubs even have built-in snowshoes! Their paws are wide and thick to protect them from ice.

Unlike other big cats, snow leopards can't roar!

BELUGA WHALE

Beluga whales live in the icy cold waters of the Arctic Ocean. At birth, beluga whale **calves** have bluish-gray coats like most other whales. As they grow, their skin fades to white. Beluga whales live in pods, where they communicate with one another through clicks and whistles. This helps in the winter, when the pods must travel to warmer waters to escape the ice.

Unlike other whales, the beluga whale can swim backward!

ARCTIC FOX

arctic foxes were born to survive in the coldest environments. Their furry paws and narrow **muzzles** are designed to help them conserve heat. When it gets too chilly, they wrap themselves with their fluffy tails just like a blanket! Arctic fox pups are born in the spring after the ice has melted. Their coats are gray when they're born, but they eventually turn white to match their snowy home.

An arctic fox's incredible hearing allows it to find its prey under the snow even before it can see it!

Lemming

Lemmings are tiny **rodents** that live in the Arctic. To stay safe and warm, lemmings build homes, called burrows, underneath the ground. The burrow has a living room, a place for lemmings to eat, and even a bathroom! The mother cares for the baby lemmings in the burrow until they are strong enough to go aboveground and survive the cold temperatures alone.

Lemming mothers give birth to an average of seven babies about six times a year!

HARP SEAL

Harp seals spend their time on land and in the water. A baby harp seal, called a pup, is born on the ice. All the mothers give birth to their pups at the same time, and the mom can tell which pup is hers by its special smell. A harp seal pup is born with a layer of **blubber** to keep it warm. After a few weeks on the ice, the pup is ready for the ocean. It will take baby steps and dip its flippers into the water before diving in!

> **Before its white fur grows in, a newborn pup is called a yellowcoat!**

WOLVERINE

a baby wolverine, called a kit, is born with snow-white fur. Eventually, the white fades to a dark brown and two blond stripes appear down its back. From birth, the wolverine has strong jaws, sharp teeth, and **retractable** claws that it uses when it needs to. These help wolverines hunt and dig their dens, which protect them in the cold winter months.

> **Wolverines are omnivores, which means they eat both meat and plants!**

WALRUS

Walruses are often called the gentle giants of the Arctic. It's hard to imagine that an animal with a long whiskery mustache and a big blubbery body could be anything but playful! Walruses are known for their two large white **tusks**, which can grow up to three feet long. They use these tusks to help pull themselves out of the water and onto the ice. This looks a little like walking, so it is known as "tooth-walking"!

A walrus can stay under water for over 30 minutes without coming up for air!

Snowy Owl

a snowy owl mother doesn't build a nest in a tree or a barn like other owls. She builds her nest on the ground, right in the snow! Snowy owl chicks are born with white feathers called "down," but it's not enough to protect them from the cold. Eventually, the chicks get new feathers that help them keep warm on their own. Then they learn to fly in the Arctic skies.

Protective snowy owl parents will even fight wolves to keep their nests safe!

penguin

It's tough to be penguin parents in Antarctica, the coldest place on Earth! Once a penguin mother lays an egg, she leaves on a long journey to find food. The father stays with the egg, balancing it on his feet and covering it with feathery skin called a brood patch. The mother returns when the chick is born and feeds it food from her journey. In the summer, the chick leaves its mother's brood patch and learns to live on its own.

Penguins are birds, but they can't fly!

GLOSSARY

Blubber: a layer of fat under the skin of a marine mammal that keeps it warm

Breed: a particular type of animal

Calves: the young of several species of marine animals such as seals and whales

Camouflage: a disguise or natural coloring that allows animals or people to hide by making them look like their surroundings

Ferocious: very dangerous and violent

Musher: a person who drives a dogsled

Muzzle: an animal's nose and mouth

Pod: a group of certain kinds of sea animals

Retractable: able to be drawn back

Rodent: a mammal with large, sharp front teeth that are used for gnawing things

Tusks: a pair of long, pointed teeth that stick out of the mouth of an animal such as a walrus

Water-repellent: resistant to water